CPS-MORRILL SCHOOL

32457127500274
921 OBA

Barack Obama

DATE DUE

921   Britton, Tamara L.,
OBA   Barack Obama

MORRILL SCHOOL
CHICAGO PUBLIC SCHOOLS
6011 S ROCKWELL ST
CHICAGO, IL 60629

The UNITED STATES PRESIDENTS

Barack

OBAMA

Tamara L. Britton

Big Buddy Books

An Imprint of Abdo Publishing
abdopublishing.com

abdopublishing.com

Published by Abdo Publishing, a division of ABDO, PO Box 398166, Minneapolis, Minnesota 55439.
Copyright © 2017 by Abdo Consulting Group, Inc. International copyrights reserved in all countries. No part of this book may be reproduced in any form without written permission from the publisher. Big Buddy Books™ is a trademark and logo of Abdo Publishing.

Printed in the United States of America, North Mankato, Minnesota
062016
092016

Design: Sarah DeYoung, Mighty Media, Inc.
Production: Mighty Media, Inc.
Editor: Paige Polinsky
Cover Photograph: Public Domain
Interior Photographs: AP Images (pp. 6, 7, 9, 11, 15, 17, 19, 27, 29); Getty Images (pp. 5, 21, 25);
    Glow Images (p. 13)

Cataloging-in-Publication Data

Names: Britton, Tamara L., author.
Title: Barack Obama / by Tamara L. Britton.
Description: Minneapolis, MN : Abdo Publishing, [2017] | Series: United States
    presidents | Includes bibliographical references and index.
Identifiers: LCCN 2015957556 | ISBN 9781680781113 (lib. bdg.) |
    ISBN 9781680775310 (ebook)
Subjects: LCSH: Obama, Barack, 1961- --Juvenile literature. | Presidents--
    United States--Biography--Juvenile literature. | United States--Politics and
    government--2009- --Juvenile literature.
Classification: DDC 973.932/092 [B]--dc23
LC record available at http://lccn.loc.gov/2015957556

Contents

Barack Obama

In 2008, Barack Obama became the forty-fourth US president. It was a historic accomplishment. No other African American had ever held the office.

Obama first served as a community leader, **lawyer**, and senator. He fought for the health and well-being of his country. And he continued to do so as president.

President Obama worked to end the wars in Iraq and Afghanistan. He fought to improve the **economy** and offered **health care** to all.

Timeline

1961

On August 4, Barack Hussein Obama Jr. was born in Honolulu, Hawaii.

2004

Obama won election to the US Senate.

1983

Obama **graduated** from Columbia **University** in New York City.

2009

Obama took office as the forty-fourth US president.

2010

In March, Obama signed the Affordable Care Act.

2015

On June 26, the **Supreme Court** made same-sex marriage **legal**.

2012

Obama was reelected president.

2014

Obama ordered **air strikes** in Syria.

Young Barry

Barack Hussein Obama Jr. was born on August 4, 1961, in Honolulu, Hawaii. His parents were Barack Sr. and Stanley "Ann" Dunham. As a boy, Barack was called Barry.

Barry's parents **divorced** in 1964. Ann later married Lolo Soetoro. In 1967, Barry, Ann, and Soetoro moved to Jakarta, Indonesia.

★ FAST FACTS ★

Born: August 4, 1961

Wife: Michelle Robinson (1964–)

Children: two

Political Party: Democrat

Age at Inauguration: 47

Years Served: 2009–2017

Vice President: Joe Biden

Barry and his
mother, Ann

School Days

When Barry was ten years old, Ann sent him back to Hawaii for school. He lived with her parents in Honolulu. There, Barry attended the respected Punahou School.

Ann returned to Hawaii in 1972. Barack Sr. visited Barry that same year. It was the last time Barry saw his father. Barack Sr. died in a car crash in 1982.

When Barry was 14 years old, Ann moved back to Indonesia. Barry stayed in Hawaii. He **graduated** from high school in 1979.

Barry and some Punahou classmates on a field trip to Tokyo, Japan

Seeking Change

After high school, Obama moved to Los Angeles, California. There, he attended Occidental College. He saw how words could be powerful tools for change.

In 1981, Obama changed schools. He moved to Columbia **University** in New York City. Obama **graduated** from Columbia two years later.

★ DID YOU KNOW? ★

In college, Obama wrote poems. They were printed in a Columbia magazine.

At Occidental, Obama lived in this room in Haines Hall.

Work and Family

Obama moved to Chicago, Illinois, in 1985. There, he found work as a community leader. Obama helped people find jobs and improve their communities.

In 1988, Obama entered Harvard Law School in Cambridge, Massachusetts. Three years later, he **graduated**. Then, he moved back to Chicago.

Obama married Michelle Robinson on October 3, 1992. The Obamas later had two daughters. Malia Ann was born in 1998. Natasha, called Sasha, was born in 2001.

(*Left to right*) Michelle, Malia, Barack, and Sasha Obama

Senator Obama

In 1992, Obama began teaching law at the **University** of Chicago. He also helped more Hispanics and African Americans vote.

Obama ran for the Illinois state senate in 1996. And he won! In the senate, Obama fought against racial **profiling**.

In 2004, Obama was elected to the US Senate. Senator Obama cowrote a bill to reduce **nuclear weapons**. He also opposed the war in Iraq.

Senator Obama worked to improve education and cut taxes for Illinois families.

17

Presidential Race

On July 27, 2004, Obama spoke at the **Democratic National Convention (DNC)** in Boston, Massachusetts. Four years later, the **Democratic** Party selected him for president.

Obama ran against **Republican** senator John McCain of Arizona. Voters wanted answers to the struggling **economy**. Many also wanted an end to the wars in Iraq and Afghanistan.

On November 4, 2008, Obama was elected the forty-fourth US president. He became the first African-American president in US history.

At the 2004 DNC, Obama called on Americans to stand together.

President Obama

Obama signed the American Recovery and Reinvestment Act on February 17, 2009. The bill helped improve the **economy**. That same year, Obama was presented the **Nobel Peace Prize**.

In March 2010, Obama signed the Affordable Care Act (ACA). It **insured** 32 million Americans. The next month, he signed an agreement with Russian president Dmitry Medvedev. This reduced **nuclear weapons**.

★ SUPREME COURT ★
APPOINTMENTS

Sonia Sotomayor: 2009

Elena Kagan: 2010

The United States and Russia hold most of the world's nuclear weapons. Medvedev (*left*) and Obama aimed to reduce that danger.

21

On December 13, 2010, Obama signed the Healthy Hunger-Free Kids Act. This law improved the National School Lunch Program. Now, lunches had to include more fruits and vegetables.

Meanwhile, the wars in the Middle East continued. Fighting troops withdrew from Iraq on August 31, 2010. But more work needed to be done in Afghanistan. So, the president sent more troops.

Then, on May 2, 2011, President Obama ordered a secret attack. Troops stormed a house in Pakistan. There, they killed **terrorist** leader Osama bin Laden.

PRESIDENT OBAMA'S CABINET

First Term
January 20, 2009–January 20, 2013

★ **STATE:** Hillary Rodham Clinton
★ **TREASURY:** Timothy F. Geithner
★ **DEFENSE:** Robert M. Gates,
   Leon E. Panetta (from July 1, 2011),
★ **ATTORNEY GENERAL:** Eric H. Holder Jr.
★ **INTERIOR:** Kenneth L. Salazar
★ **AGRICULTURE:** Thomas J. Vilsack
★ **COMMERCE:** Gary F. Locke,
   John E. Bryson (from October 21, 2011, to June 21, 2012)
★ **LABOR:** Hilda L. Solis
★ **HEALTH AND HUMAN SERVICES:**
   Kathleen Sebelius
★ **HOUSING AND URBAN DEVELOPMENT:**
   Shaun L.S. Donovan
★ **TRANSPORTATION:** Ray LaHood
★ **ENERGY:** Steven Chu
★ **EDUCATION:** Arne Duncan
★ **VETERANS AFFAIRS:** Eric K. Shinseki
★ **HOMELAND SECURITY:** Janet A. Napolitano

Second Term
January 20, 2013–January 20, 2017

★ **STATE:** Hillary Rodham Clinton,
   John Kerry (from February 1, 2013)
★ **TREASURY:** Timothy F. Geithner,
   Jack Lew (from February 28, 2013)
★ **DEFENSE:** Leon E. Panetta,
   Chuck Hagel (from February 27, 2013),
   Ashton Carter (from February 17, 2015)
★ **ATTORNEY GENERAL:** Eric H. Holder Jr.,
   Loretta E. Lynch (from April 27, 2015)
★ **INTERIOR:** Kenneth L. Salazar,
   Sally Jewell (from April 12, 2013)
★ **AGRICULTURE:** Thomas J. Vilsack
★ **COMMERCE:** Penny Pritzker (from June 26, 2013)
★ **LABOR:** Hilda L. Solis,
   Thomas E. Perez (from July 23, 2013)
★ **HEALTH AND HUMAN SERVICES:**
   Kathleen Sebelius,
   Sylvia Matthews Burwell (from June 9, 2014)
★ **HOUSING AND URBAN DEVELOPMENT:**
   Shaun L.S. Donovan,
   Julián Castro (from July 28, 2014)
★ **TRANSPORTATION:** Ray LaHood,
   Anthony Foxx (from July 2, 2013)
★ **ENERGY:** Steven Chu,
   Ernest Moniz (from May 21, 2013)
★ **EDUCATION:** Arne Duncan,
   John King (from March 14, 2016)
★ **VETERANS AFFAIRS:** Eric K. Shinseki,
   Robert McDonald (from July 29, 2014)
★ **HOMELAND SECURITY:** Janet A. Napolitano,
   Jeh Johnson (from December 23, 2013)

23

Four More Years

Obama was reelected as president on November 6, 2012. He began his second term on January 21, 2013. It would be very difficult.

During 2013, the House and Senate disagreed over the yearly US spending bill. They ran out of time to pass the bill. So, the government shut down. About 800,000 government workers were out of work from October 1 to October 16.

At this time, many Americans were upset with the ACA. Obama had said that people could keep their **health care** plans.

President Obama
and his family
greet the crowd
on the night of
his reelection.

But that fall, millions were told their plans would be ended. Obama promised to help those hurt by the misunderstanding.

More disorder began on August 9, 2014, in Ferguson, Missouri. There, African-American teenager Michael Brown was shot by a white police officer. The officer was not charged. Obama asked the city to remain calm. But **riots** broke out in August, October, and November.

Obama also faced unrest overseas. The **terrorist** group **ISIL** was harming the Middle East. ISIL posed a threat to the United States as well. In 2014, Obama ordered **air strikes** on Syria. The attacks were aimed at ISIL bases.

The Ferguson police acted
with military force. More
than 300 people were arrested
during the riots.

A Busy Time

Obama's final term had its successes, too. On June 26, 2015, the **Supreme Court** made same-sex marriage **legal** in every state. Obama was the first president to advance this cause.

In August, Obama announced the Clean Power Plan. The plan placed more limits on power plants. This was meant to make the world's air cleaner.

President Barack Obama's time in office was historic. He worked to improve public health, the US **economy**, and global peace.

On June 26, 2015, a large crowd cheered outside the Supreme Court. Obama called the decision "a victory for America."

Office of the President

Branches of Government

The US government has three branches. They are the executive, legislative, and judicial branches. Each branch has some power over the others. This is called a system of checks and balances.

★ **Executive Branch**

The executive branch enforces laws. It is made up of the president, the vice president, and the president's cabinet. The president represents the United States around the world. He or she also signs bills into law and leads the military.

★ **Legislative Branch**

The legislative branch makes laws, maintains the military, and regulates trade. It also has the power to declare war. This branch includes the Senate and the House of Representatives. Together, these two houses form Congress.

★ **Judicial Branch**

The judicial branch interprets laws. It is made up of district courts, courts of appeals, and the Supreme Court. District courts try cases. Sometimes people disagree with a trial's outcome. Then he or she may appeal. If a court of appeals supports the ruling, a person may appeal to the Supreme Court.

Qualifications for Office

To be president, a candidate must be at least 35 years old. The person must be a natural-born US citizen. He or she must also have lived in the United States for at least 14 years.

Electoral College

The US presidential election is an indirect election. Voters from each state choose electors. These electors represent their state in the Electoral College. Each elector has one electoral vote. Electors cast their vote for the candidate with the highest number of votes from people in their state. A candidate must receive the majority of Electoral College votes to win.

Term of Office

Each president may be elected to two four-year terms. The presidential election is held on the Tuesday after the first Monday in November. The president is sworn in on January 20 of the following year. At that time, he or she takes the oath of office.
It states:

> I do solemnly swear (or affirm) that I will faithfully execute the office of President of the United States, and will to the best of my ability, preserve, protect and defend the Constitution of the United States.

31

Line of Succession

The Presidential Succession Act of 1947 states who becomes president if the president cannot serve. The vice president is first in the line. Next are the Speaker of the House and the President Pro Tempore of the Senate. It may happen that none of these individuals is able to serve. Then the office falls to the president's cabinet members. They would take office in the order in which each department was created:

Secretary of State

Secretary of the Treasury

Secretary of Defense

Attorney General

Secretary of the Interior

Secretary of Agriculture

Secretary of Commerce

Secretary of Labor

Secretary of Health and Human Services

Secretary of Housing and Urban Development

Secretary of Transportation

Secretary of Energy

Secretary of Education

Secretary of Veterans Affairs

Secretary of Homeland Security

Benefits

★ While in office, the president receives a salary. It is $400,000 per year. He or she lives in the White House. The president also has 24-hour Secret Service protection.

★ The president may travel on a Boeing 747 jet. This special jet is called Air Force One. It can hold 70 passengers. It has kitchens, a dining room, sleeping areas, and more. Air Force One can fly halfway around the world before needing to refuel. It can even refuel in flight!

★ When the president travels by car, he or she uses Cadillac One. It is a Cadillac Deville that has been modified. The car has heavy armor and communications systems. The president may even take Cadillac One along when visiting other countries.

★ The president also travels on a helicopter. It is called Marine One. It may also be taken along when the president visits other countries.

★ Sometimes the president needs to get away with family and friends. Camp David is the official presidential retreat. It is located in Maryland. The US Navy maintains the retreat. The US Marine Corps keeps it secure. The camp offers swimming, tennis, golf, and hiking.

★ When the president leaves office, he or she receives lifetime Secret Service protection. He or she also receives a yearly pension of $203,700. The former president also receives money for office space, supplies, and staff.

33

PRESIDENTS AND THEIR TERMS

PRESIDENT	PARTY	TOOK OFFICE	LEFT OFFICE	TERMS SERVED	VICE PRESIDENT
George Washington	None	April 30, 1789	March 4, 1797	Two	John Adams
John Adams	Federalist	March 4, 1797	March 4, 1801	One	Thomas Jefferson
Thomas Jefferson	Democratic-Republican	March 4, 1801	March 4, 1809	Two	Aaron Burr, George Clinton
James Madison	Democratic-Republican	March 4, 1809	March 4, 1817	Two	George Clinton, Elbridge Gerry
James Monroe	Democratic-Republican	March 4, 1817	March 4, 1825	Two	Daniel D. Tompkins
John Quincy Adams	Democratic-Republican	March 4, 1825	March 4, 1829	One	John C. Calhoun
Andrew Jackson	Democrat	March 4, 1829	March 4, 1837	Two	John C. Calhoun, Martin Van Buren
Martin Van Buren	Democrat	March 4, 1837	March 4, 1841	One	Richard M. Johnson
William H. Harrison	Whig	March 4, 1841	April 4, 1841	Died During First Term	John Tyler
John Tyler	Whig	April 6, 1841	March 4, 1845	Completed Harrison's Term	Office Vacant
James K. Polk	Democrat	March 4, 1845	March 4, 1849	One	George M. Dallas
Zachary Taylor	Whig	March 5, 1849	July 9, 1850	Died During First Term	Millard Fillmore

PRESIDENT	PARTY	TOOK OFFICE	LEFT OFFICE	TERMS SERVED	VICE PRESIDENT
Millard Fillmore	Whig	July 10, 1850	March 4, 1853	Completed Taylor's Term	Office Vacant
Franklin Pierce	Democrat	March 4, 1853	March 4, 1857	One	William R.D. King
James Buchanan	Democrat	March 4, 1857	March 4, 1861	One	John C. Breckinridge
Abraham Lincoln	Republican	March 4, 1861	April 15, 1865	Served One Term, Died During Second Term	Hannibal Hamlin, Andrew Johnson
Andrew Johnson	Democrat	April 15, 1865	March 4, 1869	Completed Lincoln's Second Term	Office Vacant
Ulysses S. Grant	Republican	March 4, 1869	March 4, 1877	Two	Schuyler Colfax, Henry Wilson
Rutherford B. Hayes	Republican	March 3, 1877	March 4, 1881	One	William A. Wheeler
James A. Garfield	Republican	March 4, 1881	September 19, 1881	Died During First Term	Chester Arthur
Chester Arthur	Republican	September 20, 1881	March 4, 1885	Completed Garfield's Term	Office Vacant
Grover Cleveland	Democrat	March 4, 1885	March 4, 1889	One	Thomas A. Hendricks
Benjamin Harrison	Republican	March 4, 1889	March 4, 1893	One	Levi P. Morton
Grover Cleveland	Democrat	March 4, 1893	March 4, 1897	One	Adlai E. Stevenson
William McKinley	Republican	March 4, 1897	September 14, 1901	Served One Term, Died During Second Term	Garret A. Hobart, Theodore Roosevelt

PRESIDENT	PARTY	TOOK OFFICE	LEFT OFFICE	TERMS SERVED	VICE PRESIDENT
Theodore Roosevelt	Republican	September 14, 1901	March 4, 1909	Completed McKinley's Second Term, Served One Term	Office Vacant, Charles Fairbanks
William Taft	Republican	March 4, 1909	March 4, 1913	One	James S. Sherman
Woodrow Wilson	Democrat	March 4, 1913	March 4, 1921	Two	Thomas R. Marshall
Warren G. Harding	Republican	March 4, 1921	August 2, 1923	Died During First Term	Calvin Coolidge
Calvin Coolidge	Republican	August 3, 1923	March 4, 1929	Completed Harding's Term, Served One Term	Office Vacant, Charles Dawes
Herbert Hoover	Republican	March 4, 1929	March 4, 1933	One	Charles Curtis
Franklin D. Roosevelt	Democrat	March 4, 1933	April 12, 1945	Served Three Terms, Died During Fourth Term	John Nance Garner, Henry A. Wallace, Harry S. Truman
Harry S. Truman	Democrat	April 12, 1945	January 20, 1953	Completed Roosevelt's Fourth Term, Served One Term	Office Vacant, Alben Barkley
Dwight D. Eisenhower	Republican	January 20, 1953	January 20, 1961	Two	Richard Nixon
John F. Kennedy	Democrat	January 20, 1961	November 22, 1963	Died During First Term	Lyndon B. Johnson
Lyndon B. Johnson	Democrat	November 22, 1963	January 20, 1969	Completed Kennedy's Term, Served One Term	Office Vacant, Hubert H. Humphrey
Richard Nixon	Republican	January 20, 1969	August 9, 1974	Completed First Term, Resigned During Second Term	Spiro T. Agnew, Gerald Ford

PRESIDENT	PARTY	TOOK OFFICE	LEFT OFFICE	TERMS SERVED	VICE PRESIDENT
Gerald Ford	Republican	August 9, 1974	January 20, 1977	Completed Nixon's Second Term	Nelson A. Rockefeller
Jimmy Carter	Democrat	January 20, 1977	January 20, 1981	One	Walter Mondale
Ronald Reagan	Republican	January 20, 1981	January 20, 1989	Two	George H.W. Bush
George H.W. Bush	Republican	January 20, 1989	January 20, 1993	One	Dan Quayle
Bill Clinton	Democrat	January 20, 1993	January 20, 2001	Two	Al Gore
George W. Bush	Republican	January 20, 2001	January 20, 2009	Two	Dick Cheney
Barack Obama	Democrat	January 20, 2009	January 20, 2017	Two	Joe Biden

"We do not believe that in this country, freedom is reserved for the lucky, or happiness for the few." Barack Obama

★ WRITE TO THE PRESIDENT ★

You may write to the president at:
The White House
1600 Pennsylvania Avenue NW
Washington, DC 20500

You may e-mail the president at:
comments@whitehouse.gov

37

Glossary

air strike—an attack in which military airplanes drop explosive weapons.

Democratic—relating to the Democratic political party. Democrats believe in social change and strong government.

Democratic National Convention—a meeting during which the Democratic Party chooses candidates for president and vice president.

divorce—to officially end a marriage.

economy—the way that a country produces, sells, and buys goods and services.

graduate (GRA-juh-wayt)—to complete a level of schooling.

health care—the prevention or treatment of illness by professionals.

insure—to provide insurance. Insurance is a contract that promises to guard people against a loss of money if something happens to them or their property.

ISIL—Islamic State of Iraq and the Levant. A terrorist group in Iraq and Syria.

lawyer (LAW-yuhr)—a person who gives people advice on laws or represents them in court.

legal—based on or allowed by law.

Nobel Peace Prize—an award given for doing something to help make peace in the world.

nuclear weapon—a weapon that uses the power created by splitting atoms.

profiling—the act of suspecting or targeting a person based on behavior or observed characteristics, such as race.

Republican—a member of the Republican political party.

riot—sometimes violent disorder caused by a large group of people.

Supreme Court—the highest, most powerful court of a nation or a state.

terrorist—a person who uses violence to scare or control people or governments.

university—a school a student may attend after finishing high school. A university is often made up of several colleges.

★ WEBSITES ★

To learn more about the US Presidents, visit **booklinks.abdopublishing.com**. These links are routinely monitored and updated to provide the most current information available.

Index